We can do it! Feminart is a coloring book which centers around quotes from powerful ladies throughout history. The fight for equality can be exhausting, and sometimes you just want to color in the message, as opposed to scream it from the rooftops. But after you put the pencil down, get out there and fight. This is just a break that will hopefully motivate everyone to fight for equal treatment for all. Relax and color 20 pages filled with girl power. Persistent women will always make herstory.

Sketches

Sketches

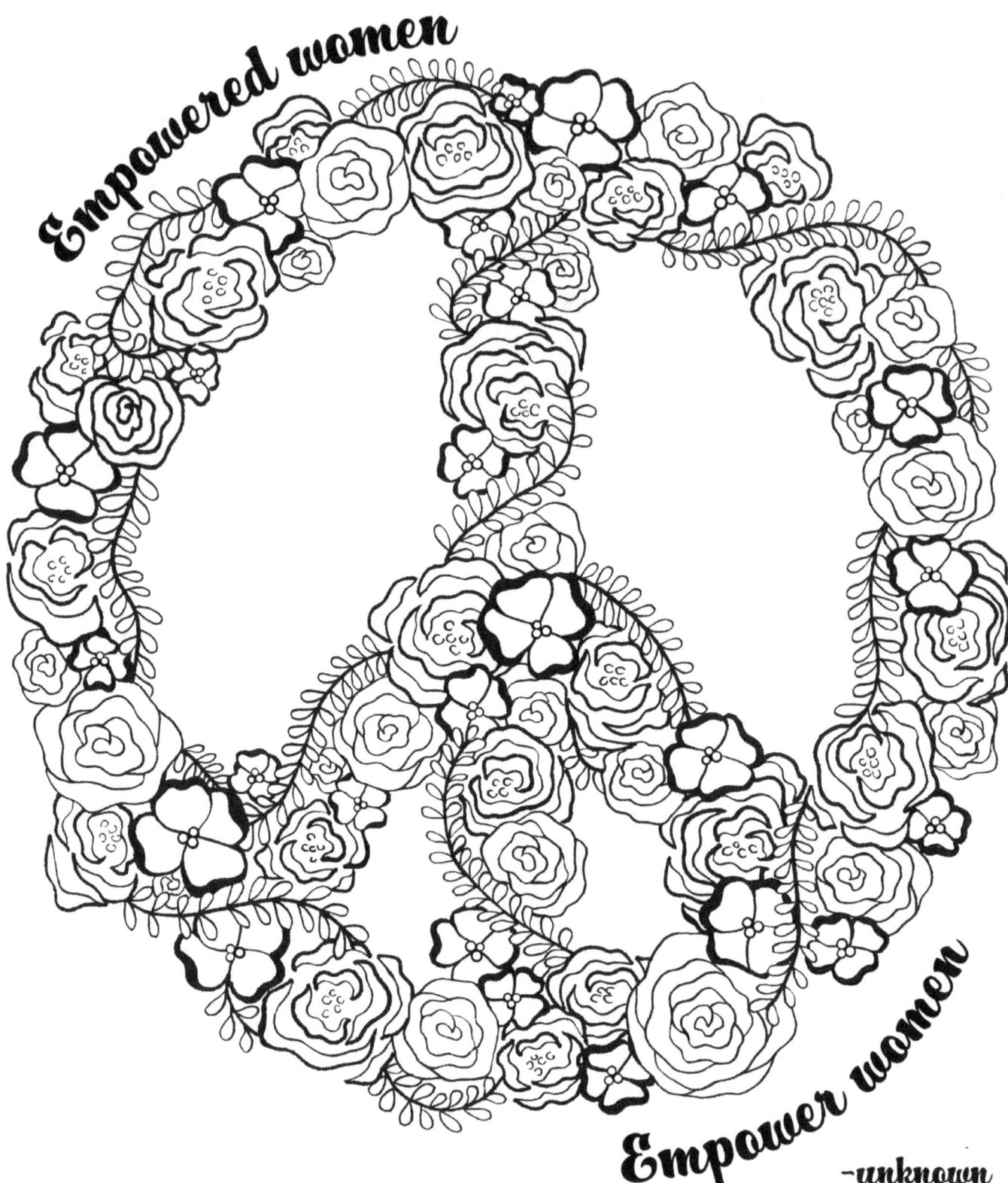

Empowered women

Empower women

-unknown

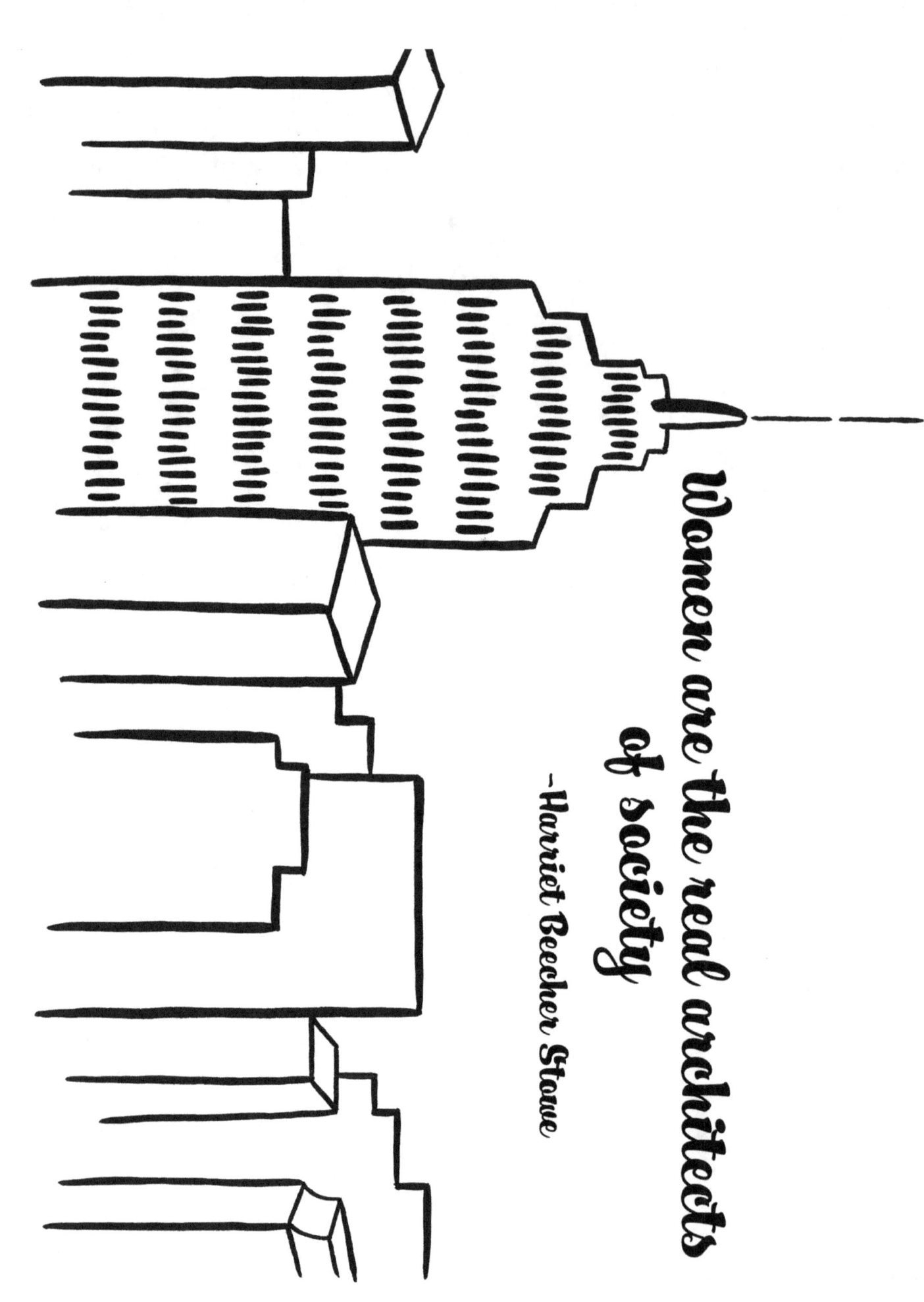

Women are the real architects of society

-Harriet Beecher Stowe

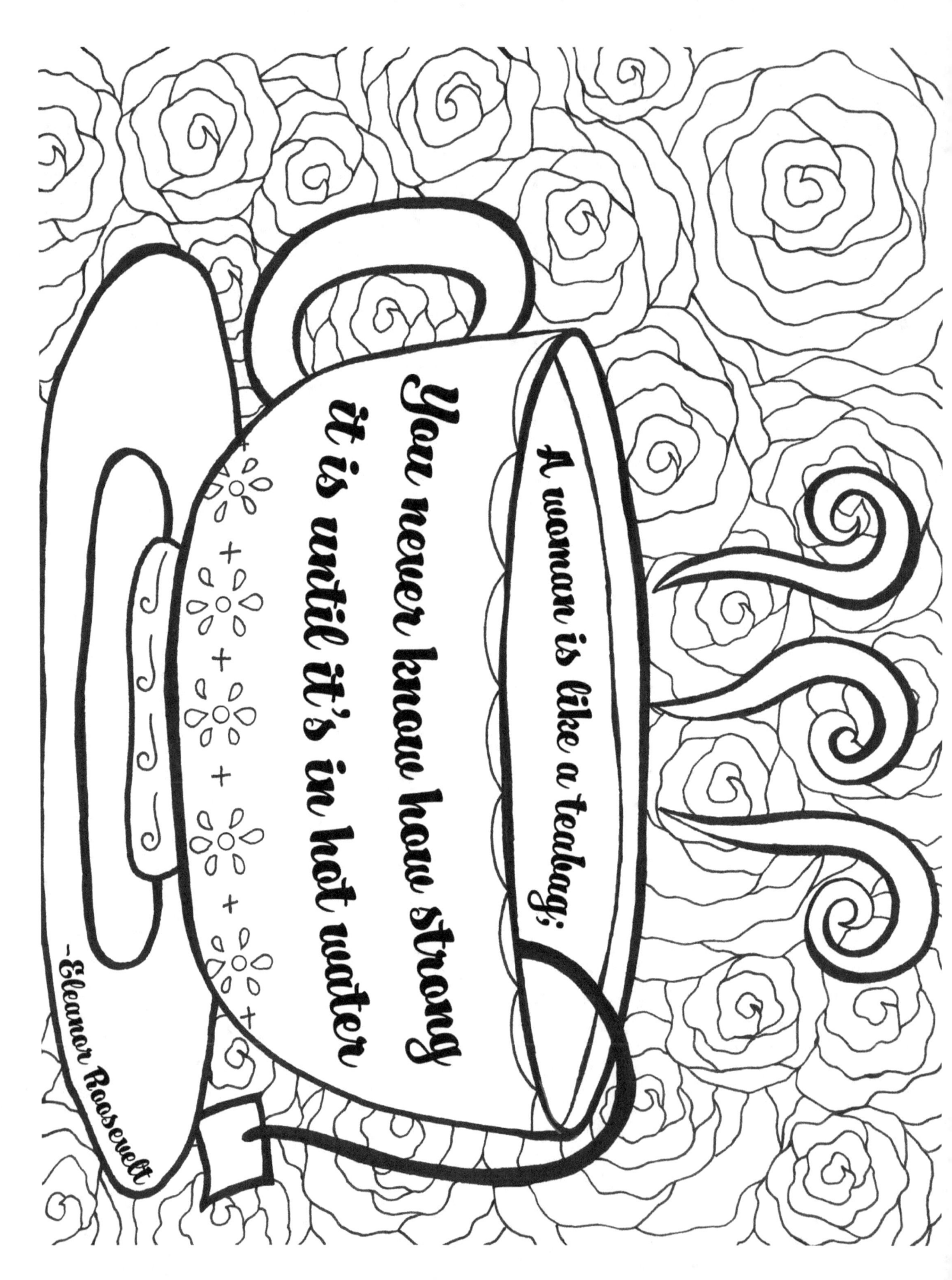

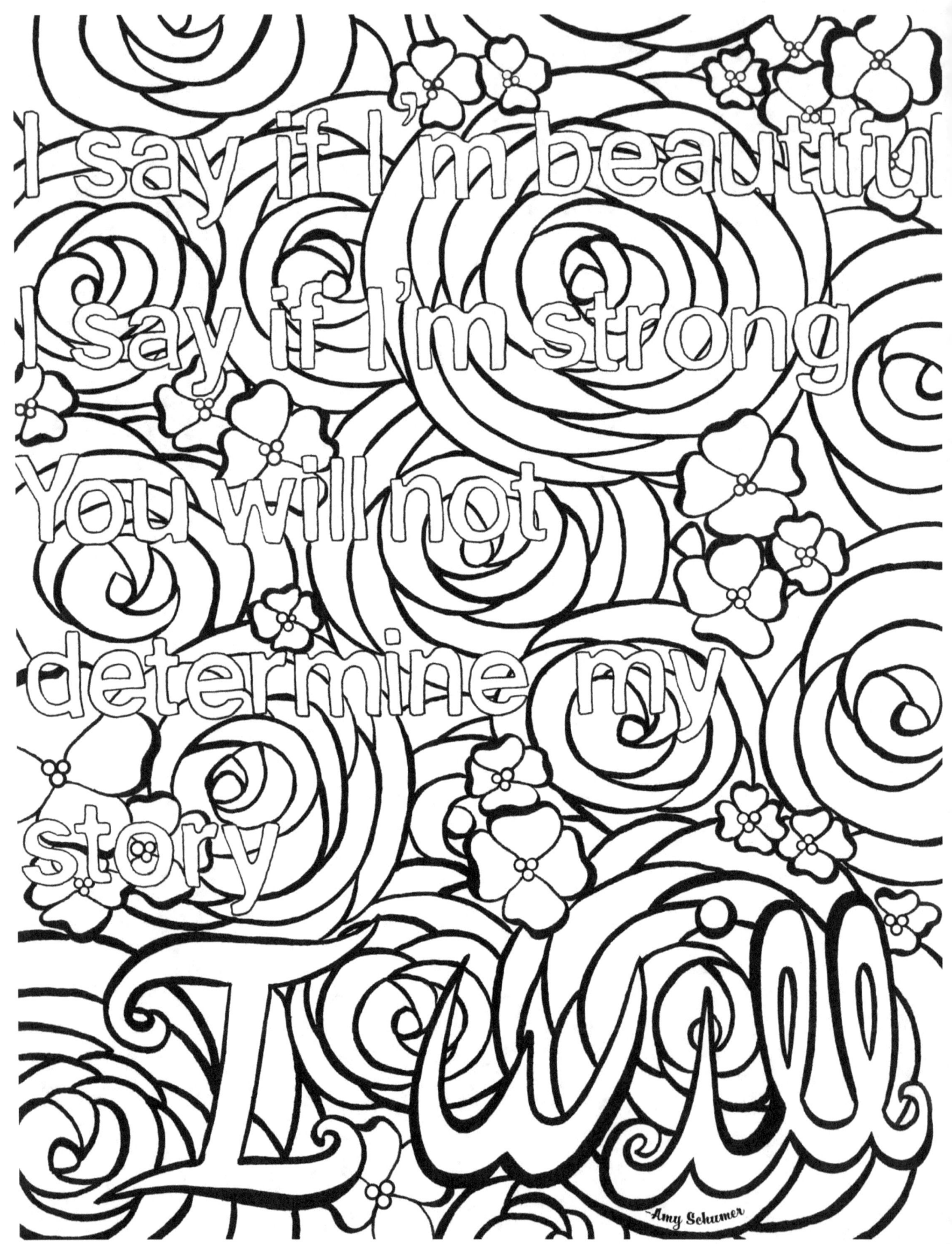

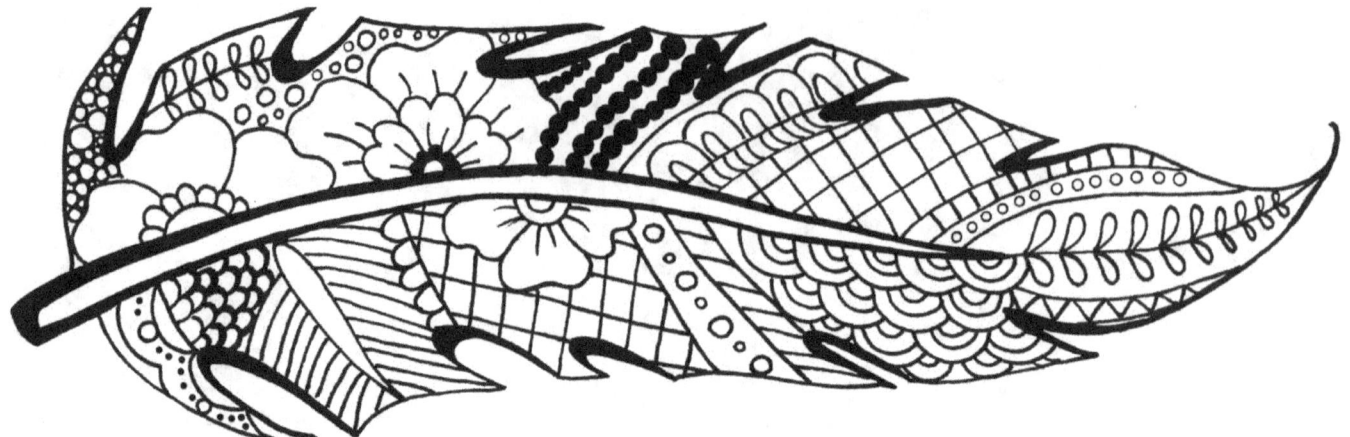

Girls compete,

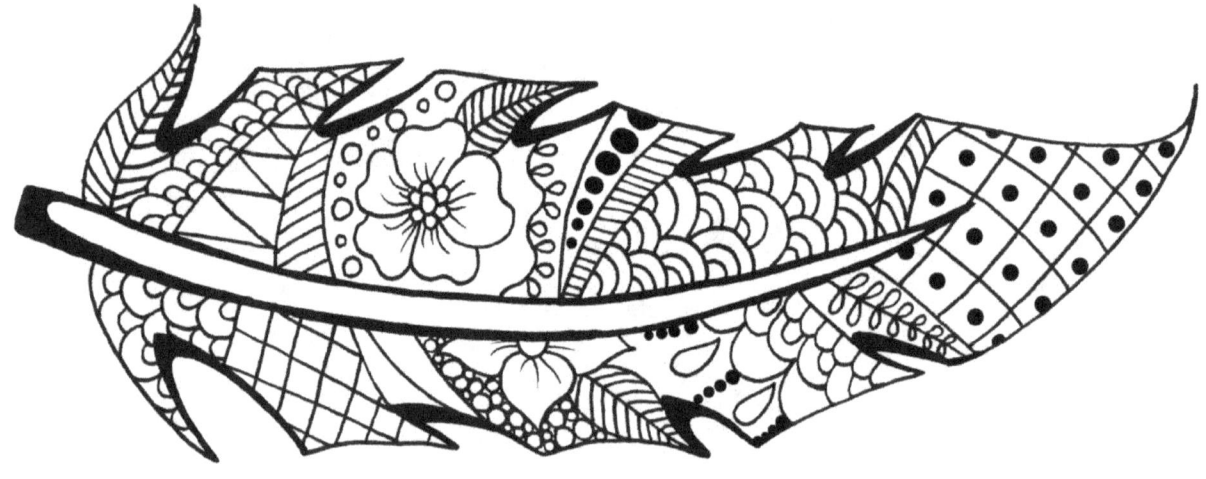

Women Empower.

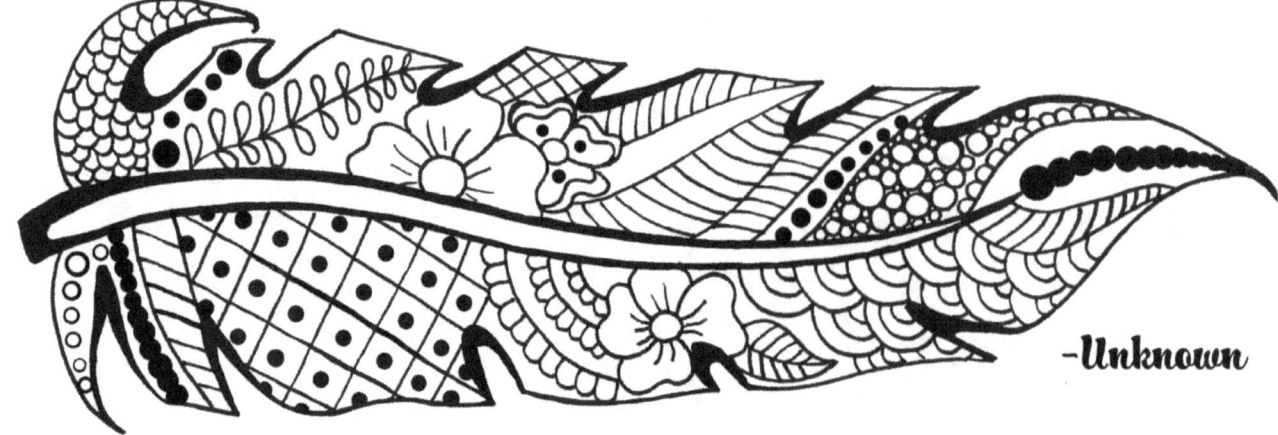

-Unknown

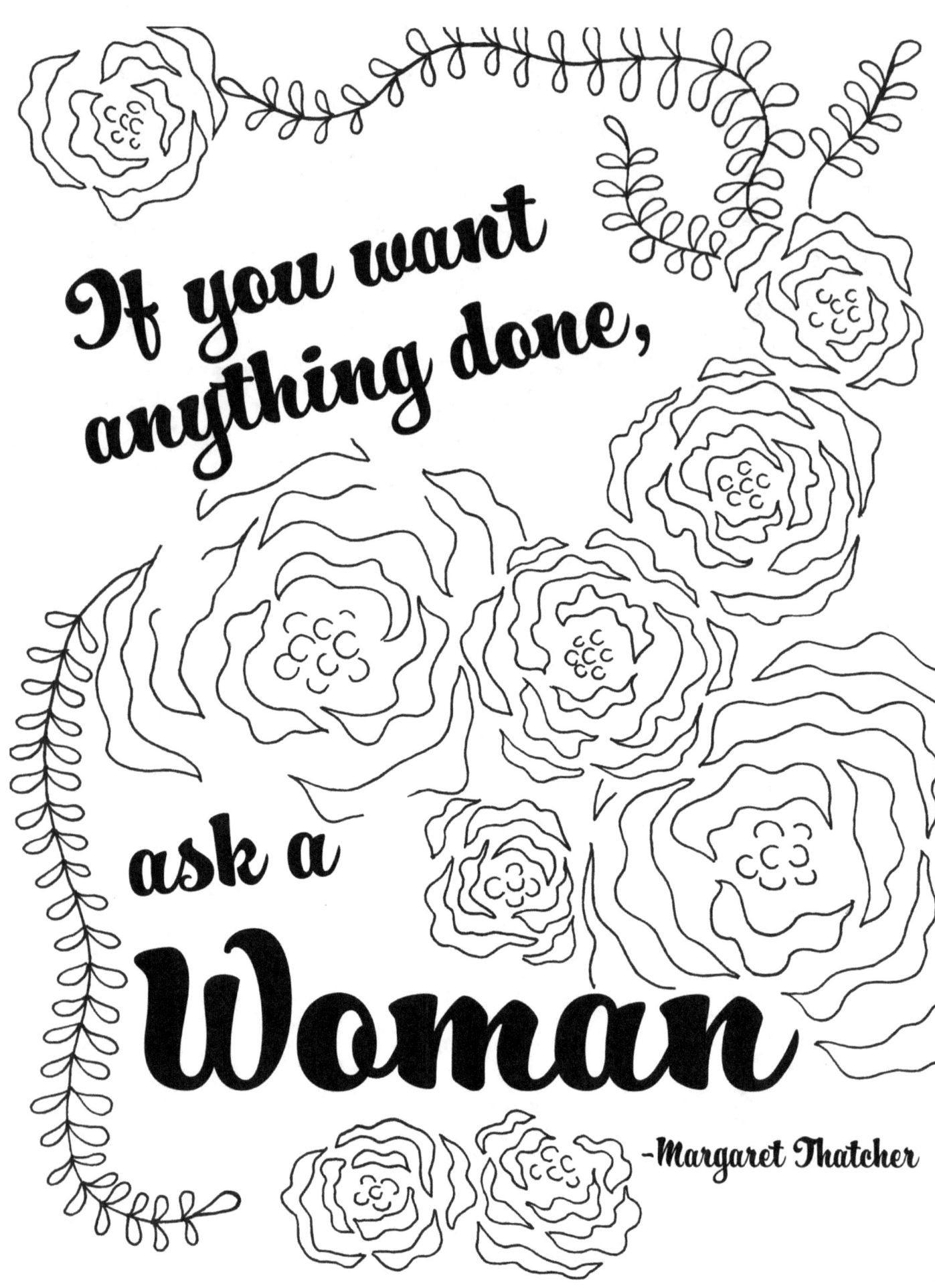

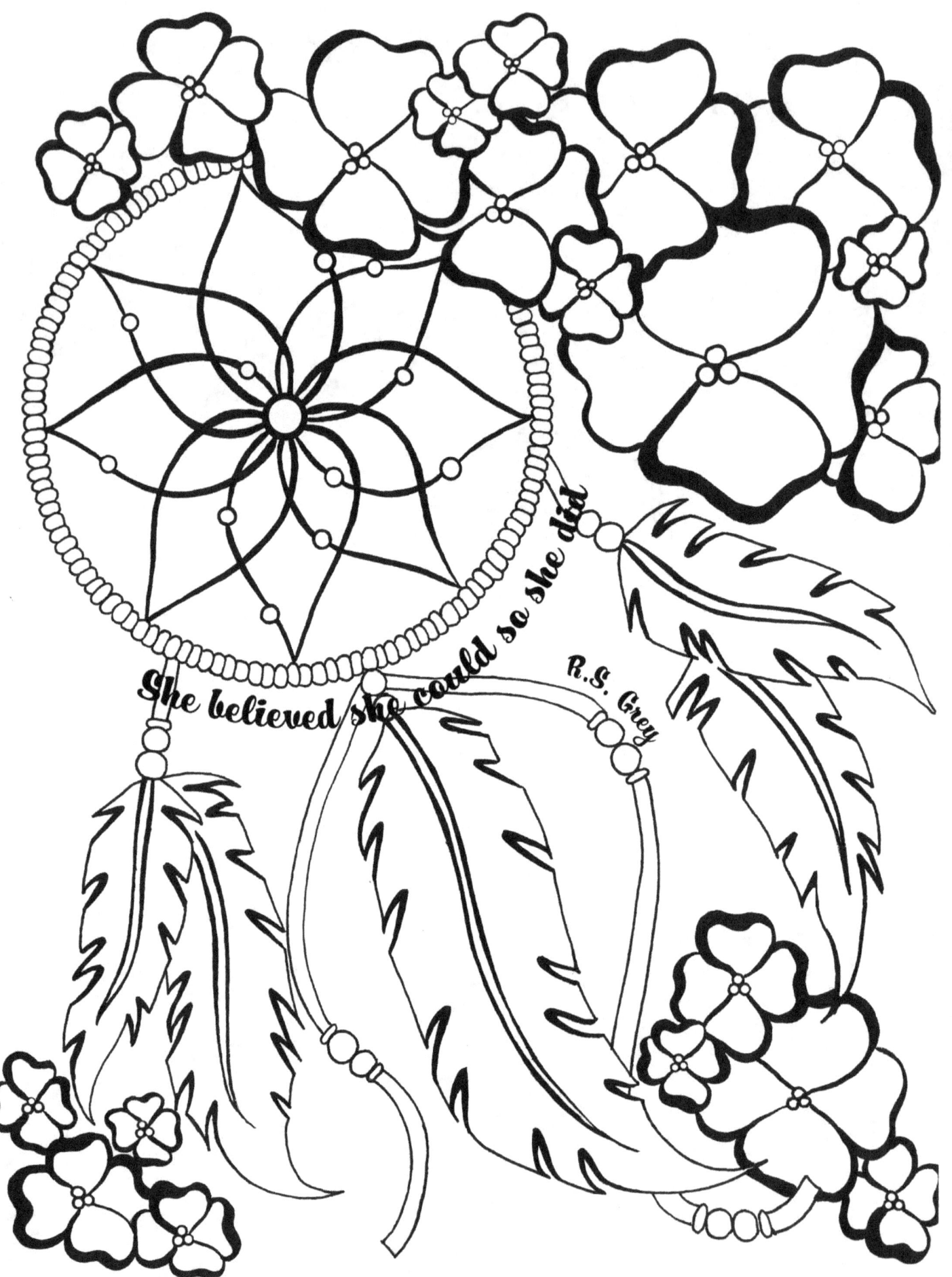

FOR MOST OF HISTORY

anonymous

WAS A WOMAN

-VIRGINIA WOOLF

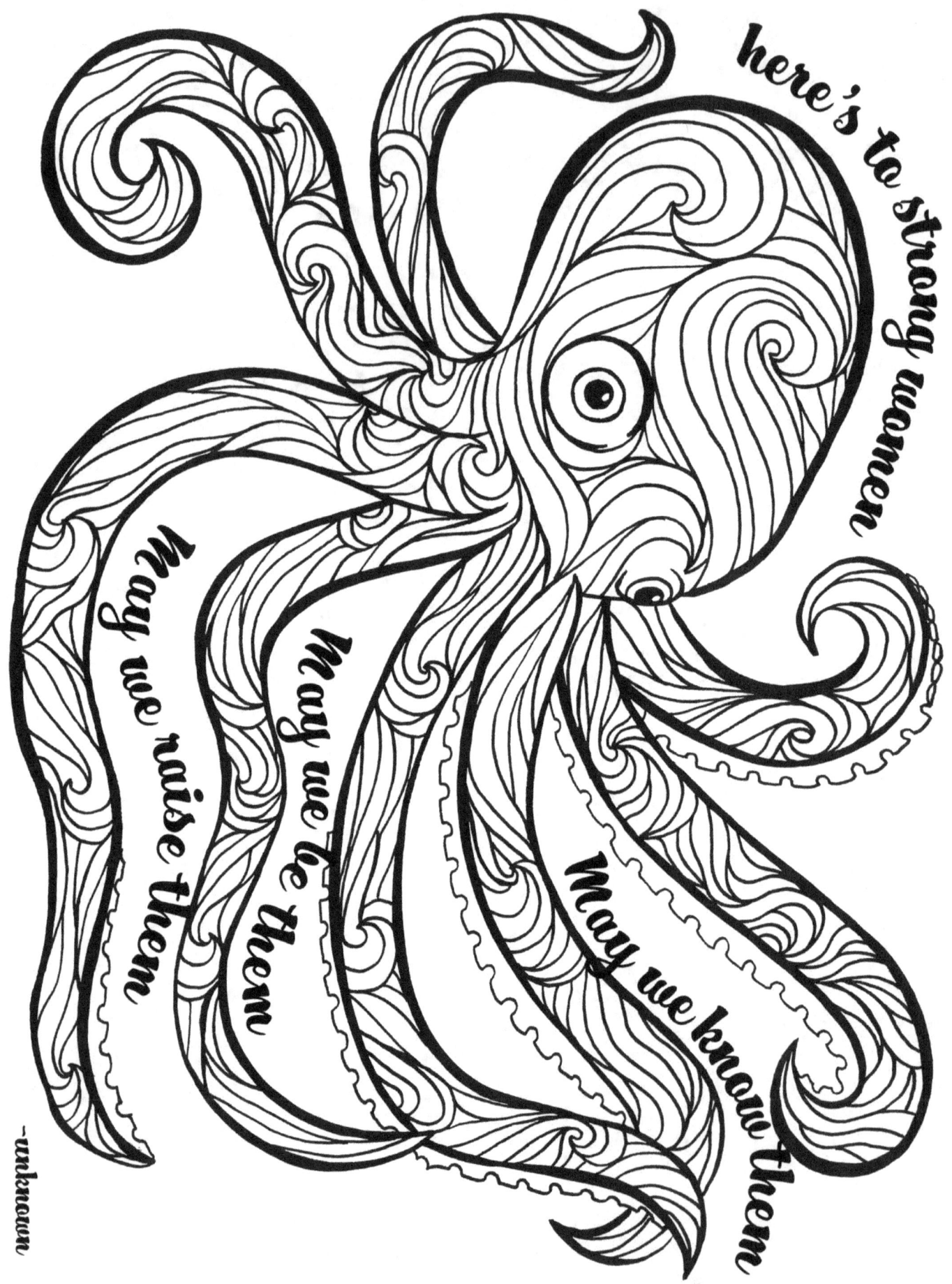

here's to strong women

May we raise them

May we be them

May we know them

-unknown

IT SHOULDN'T

BE THAT WOMEN

ARE THE EXCEPTION

-RUTH BADER GINSBURG

Women belong in all places where decisions are being made....

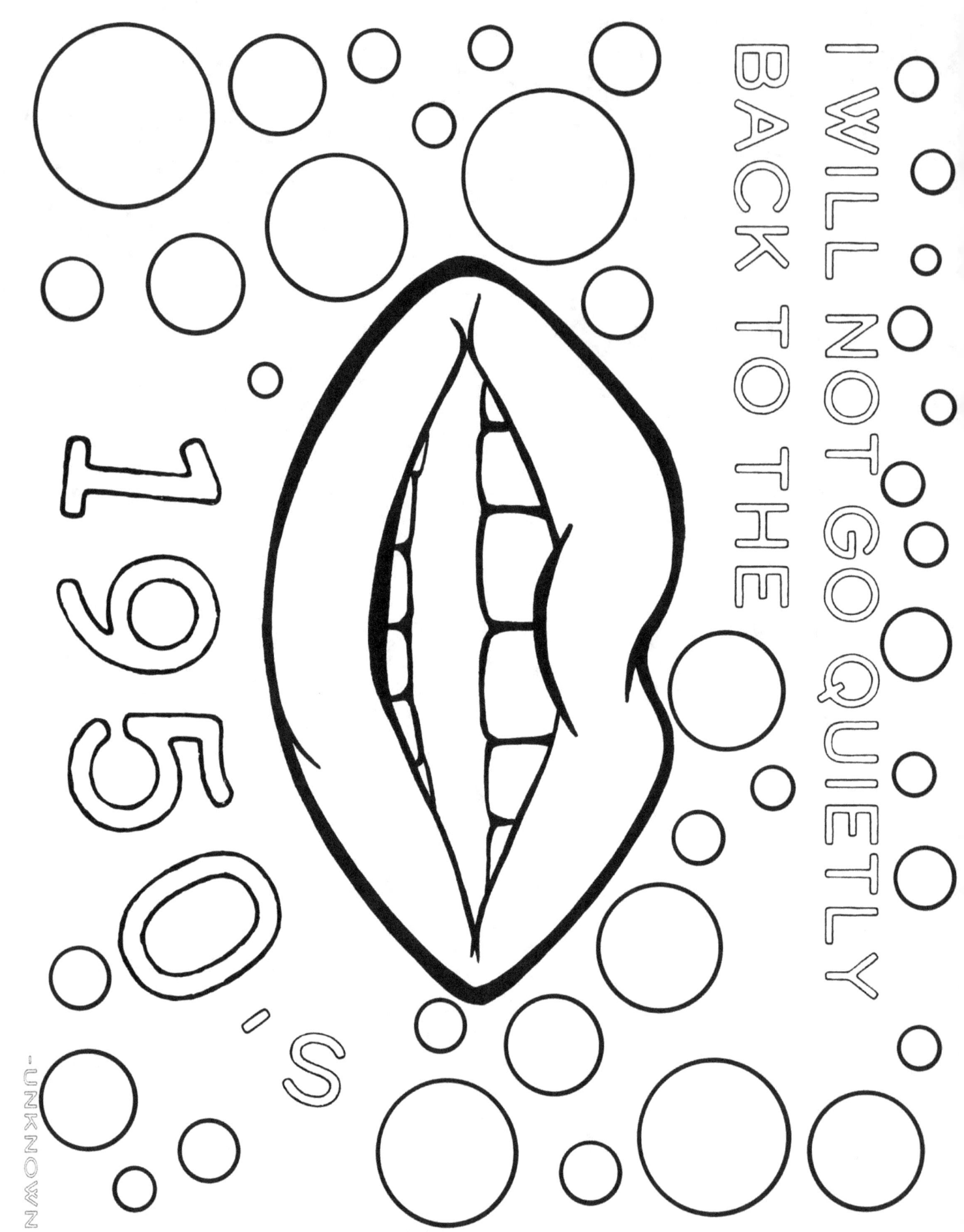

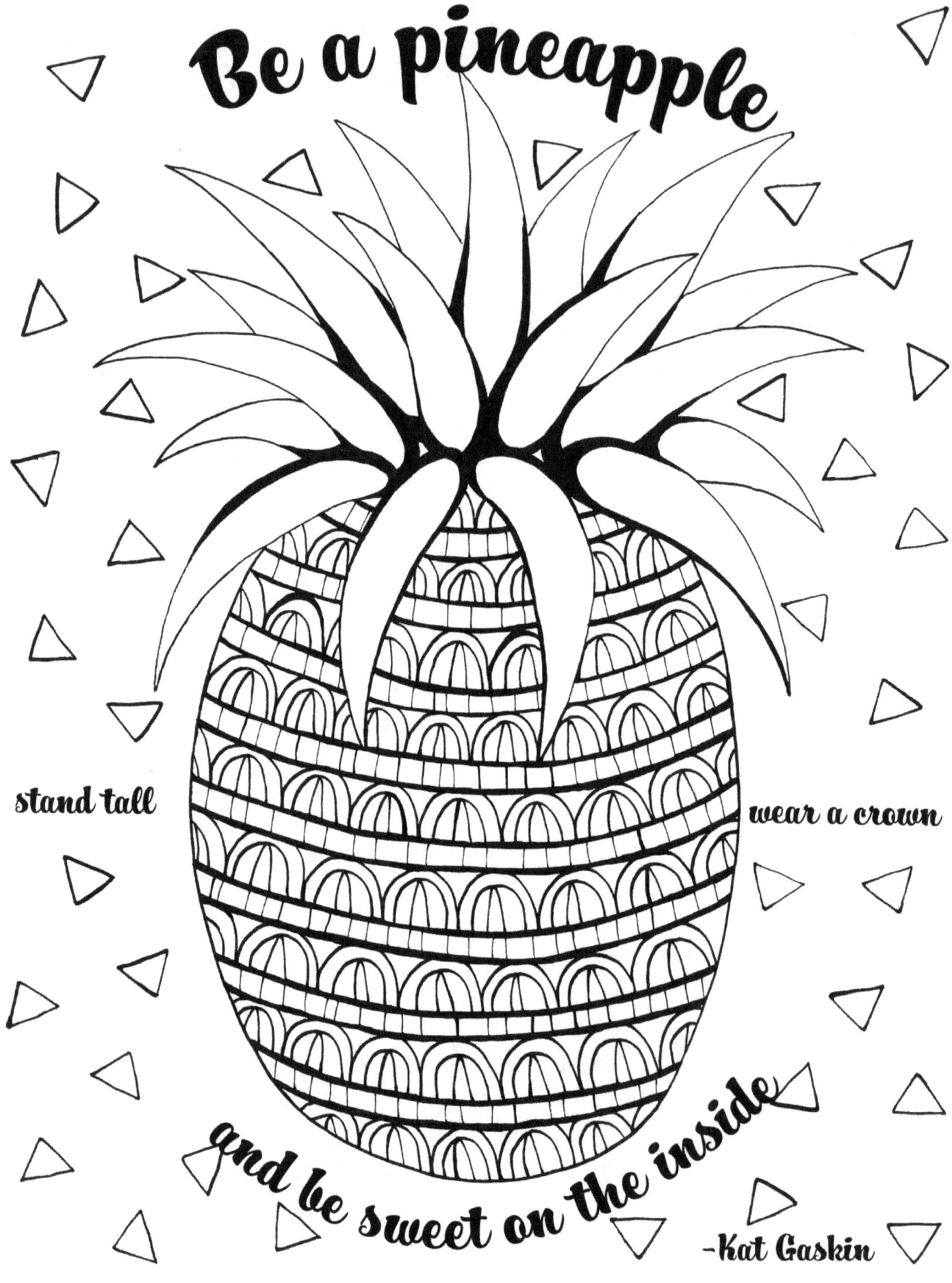

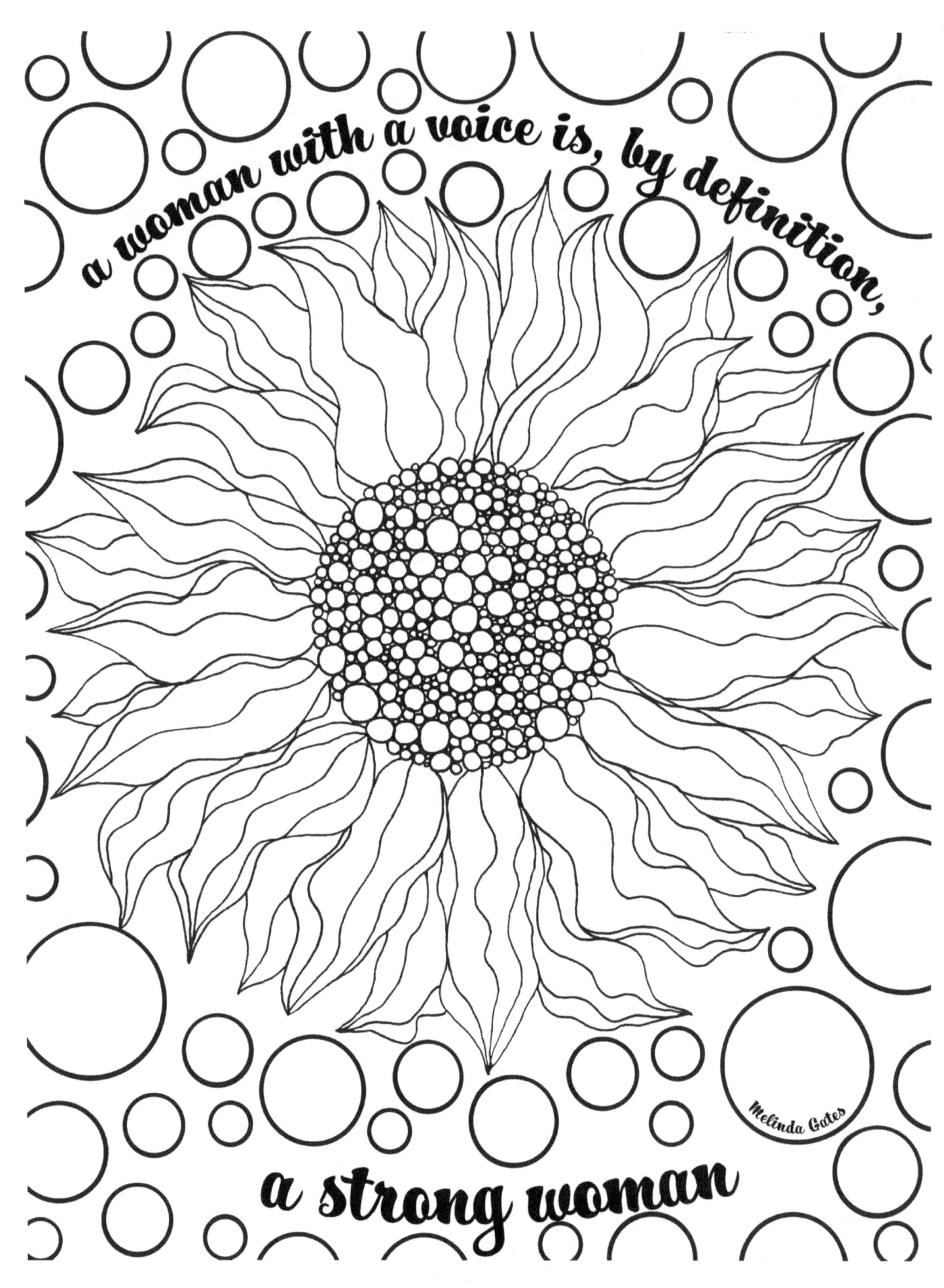

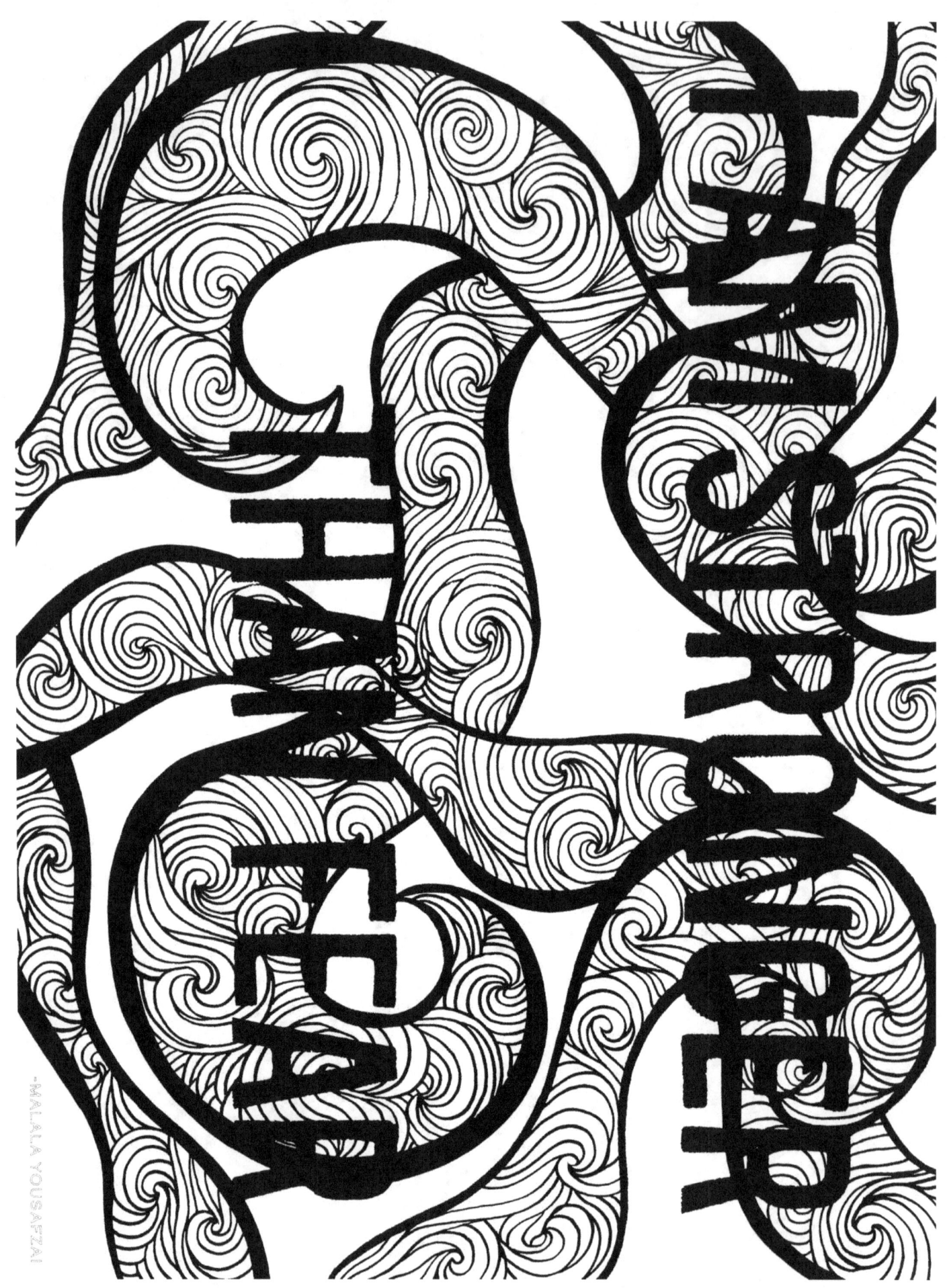

ONE CHILD, ONE TEACHER, ONE BOOK, ONE PEN CAN CHANGE THE WORLD.

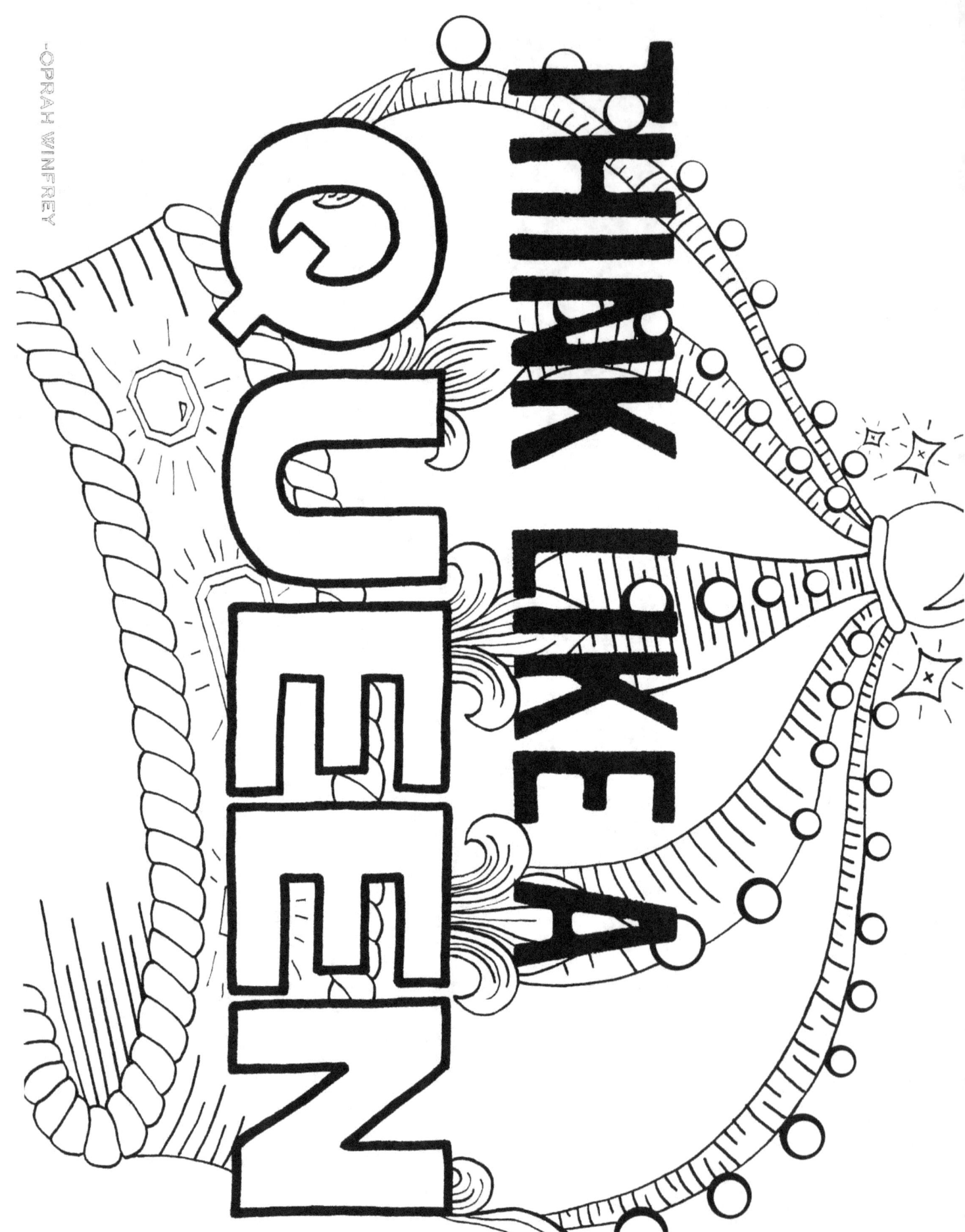

THINK LIKE A QUEEN

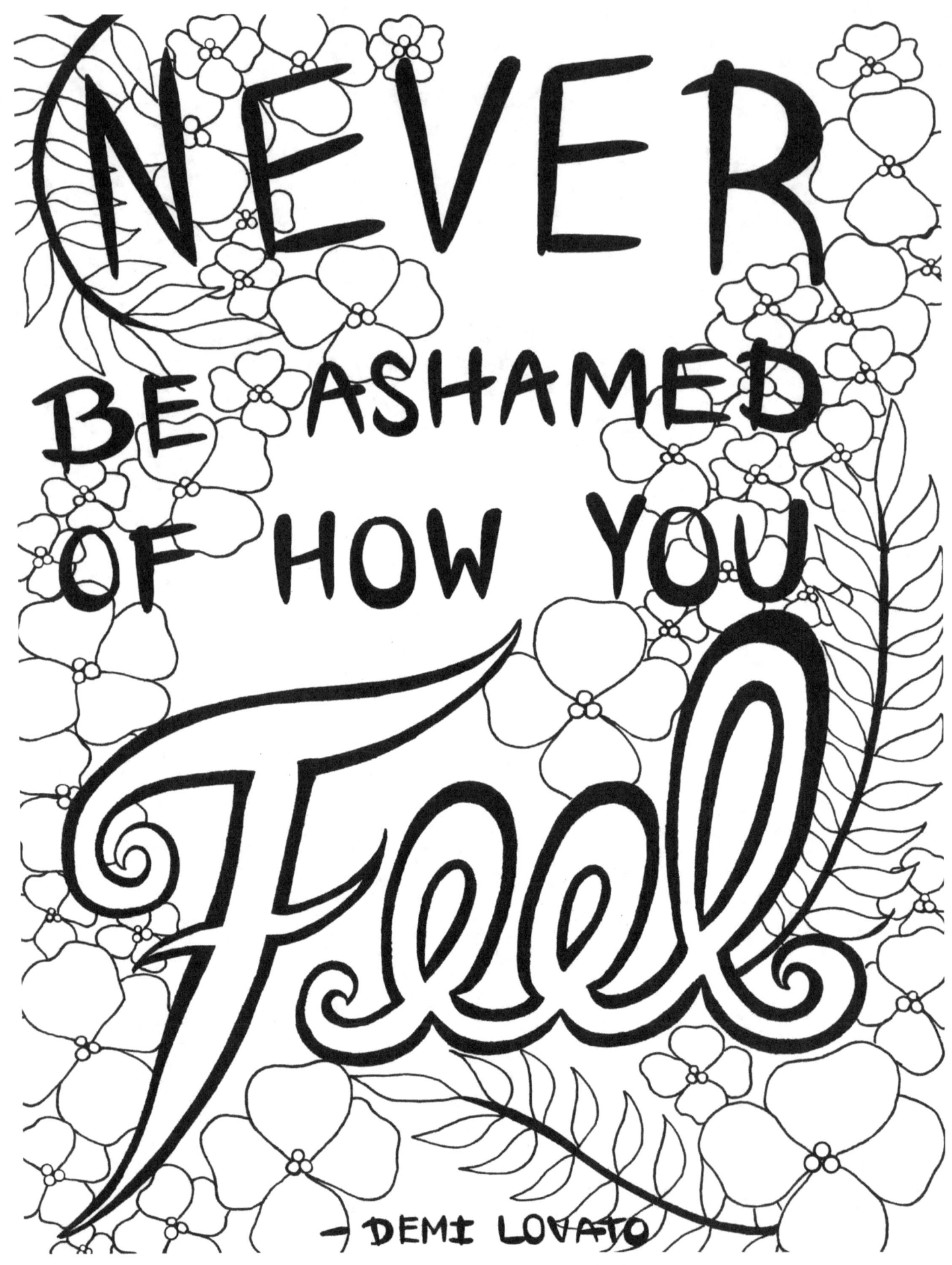

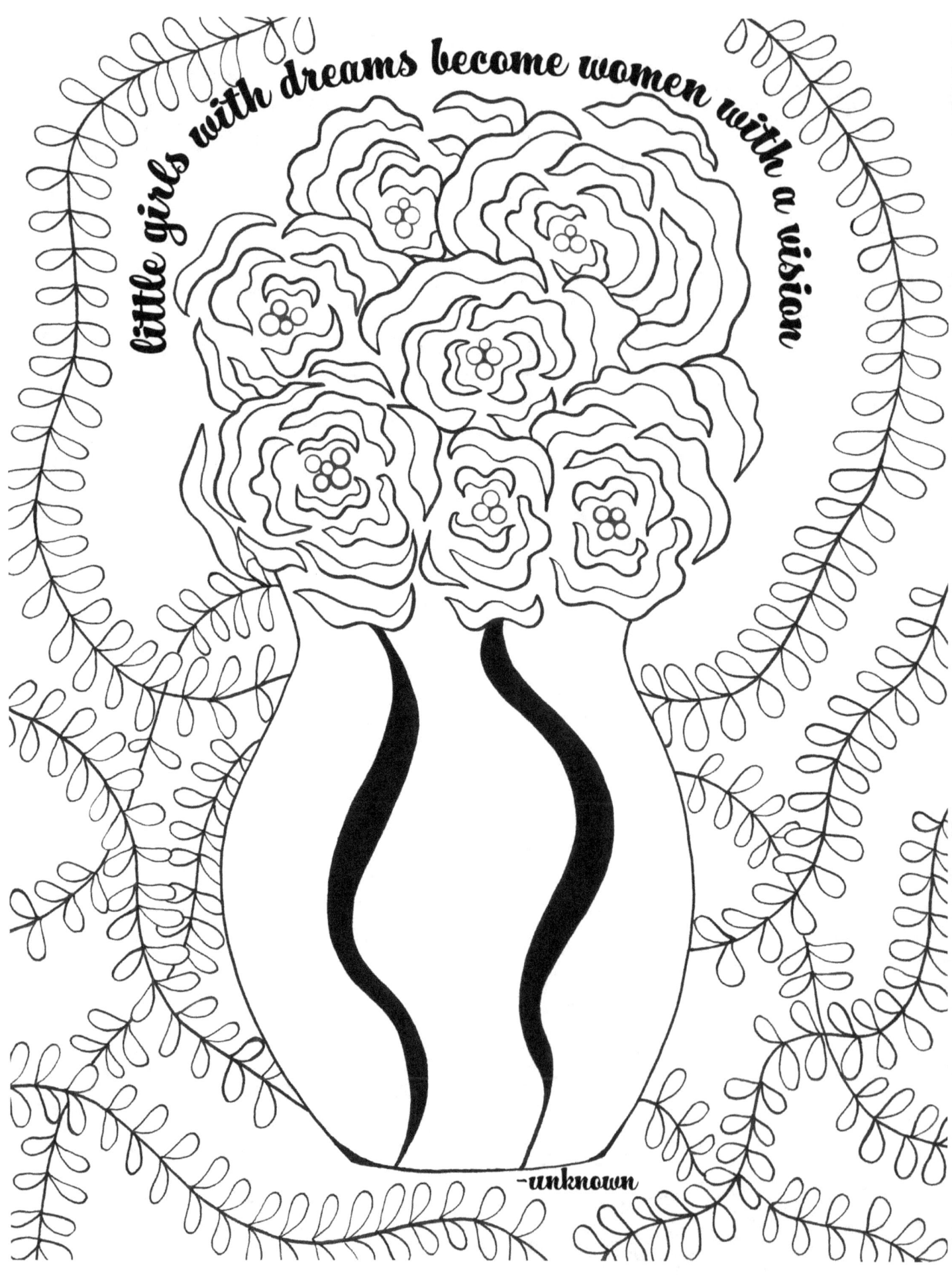

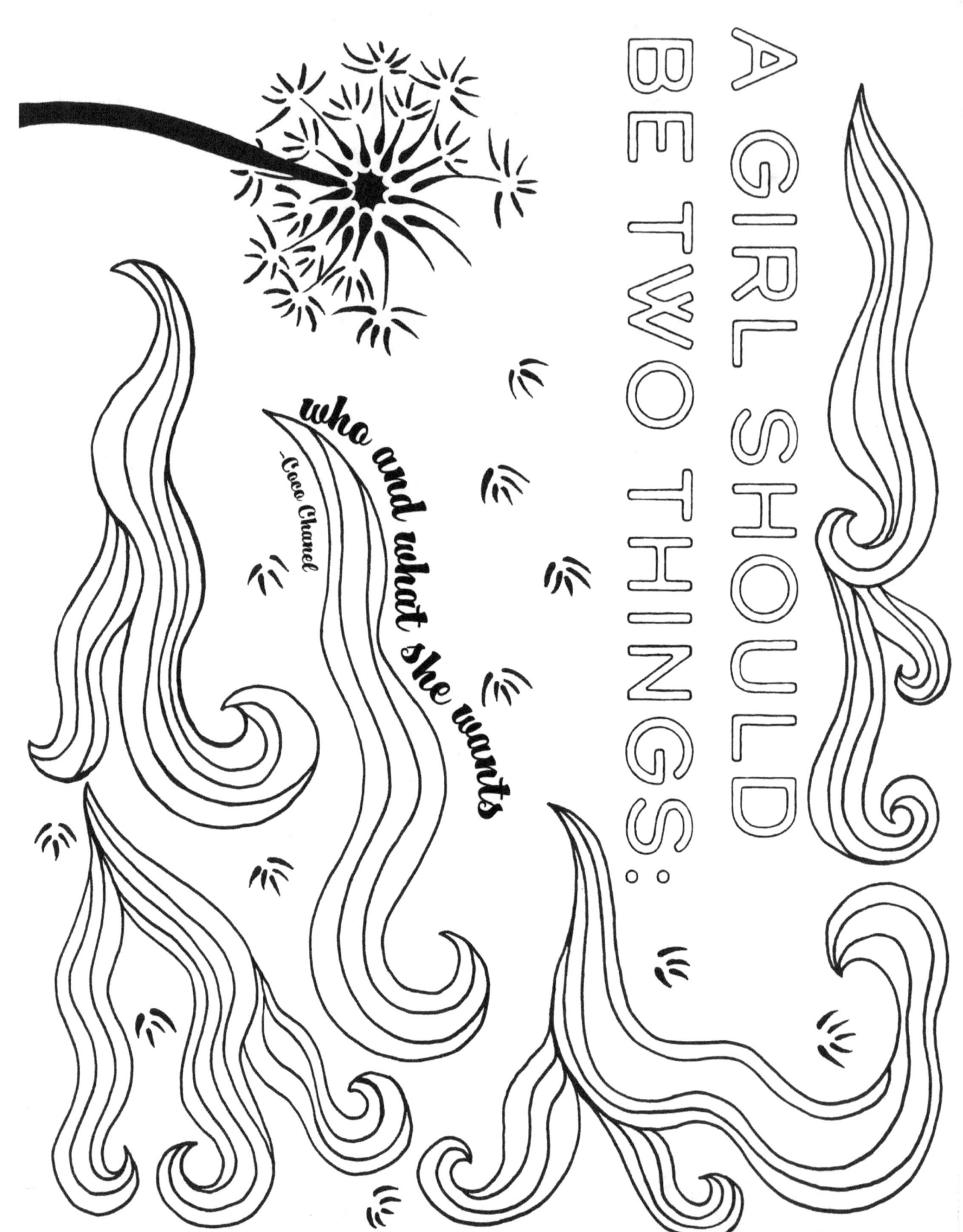

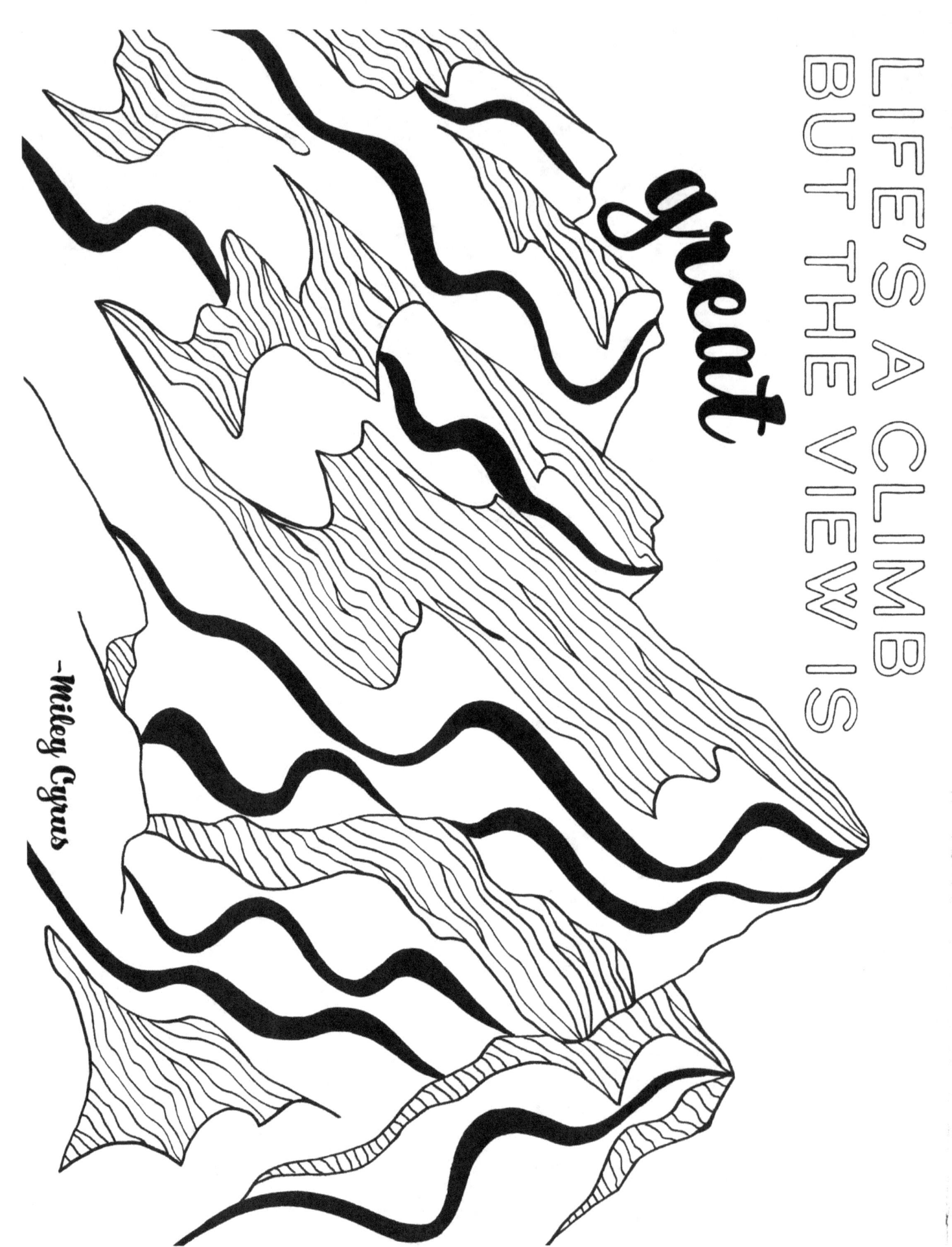

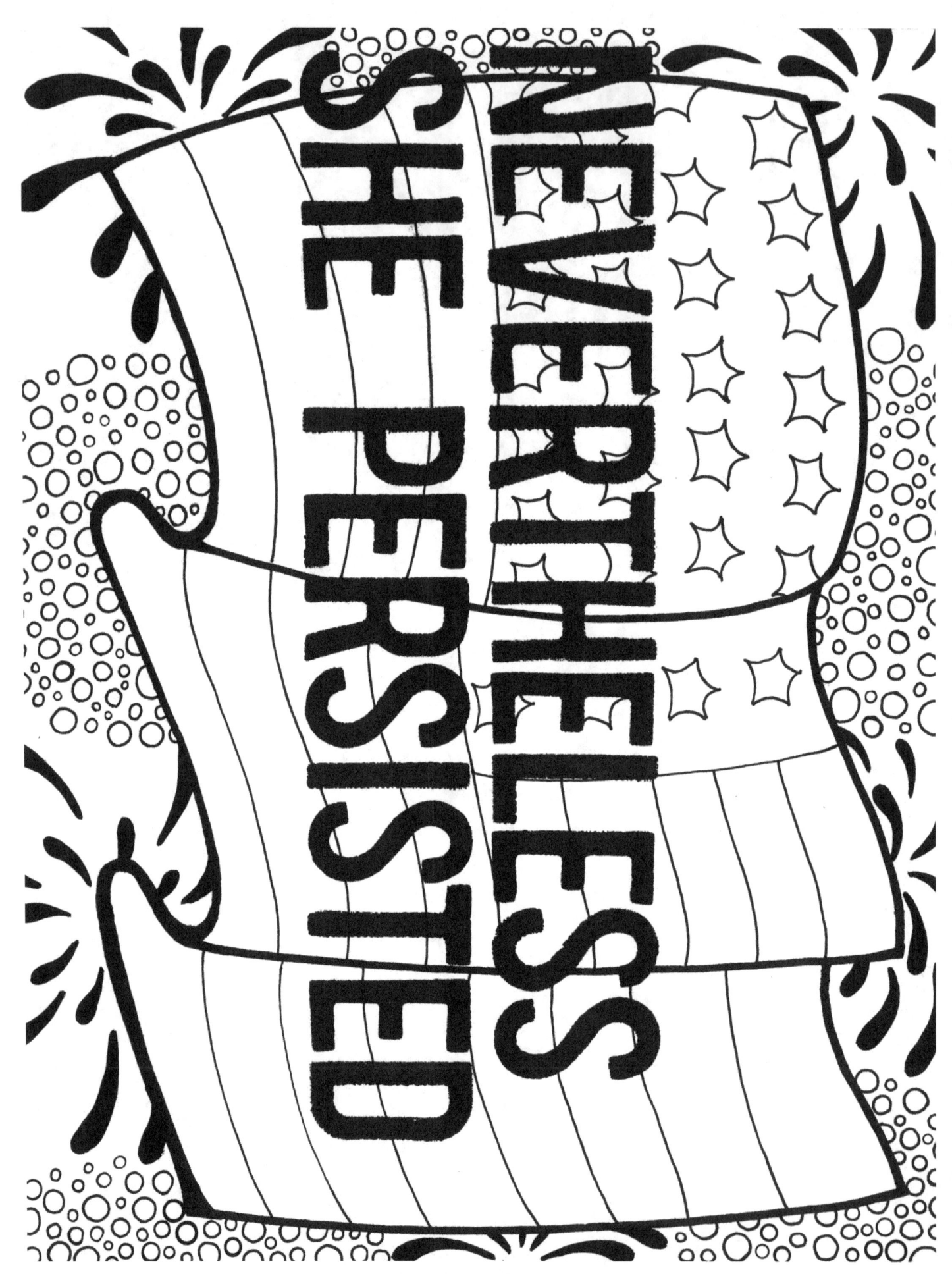